D1614929

BUT A PASSAGE IN WILDERNESS

But a Passage in Wilderness

MARGO BERDESHEVSKY

THE SHEEP MEADOW PRESS
RIVERDALE-ON-HUDSON, NEW YORK

All inquiries and permission requests should be addressed to:
The Sheep Meadow Press
P.O. Box 1345
Riverdale-on-Hudson, NY 10471

Designed and typeset by Jean-Marc Eldin
Distributed by The University Press of New England.

Printed on acid-free paper in the United States. This book meets the guidelines for permanence and durability of the Committee on Production Guidelines for Book Longevity of the Council on Library Resources.

Library of Congress Cataloging-in-Publication Data

Berdeshevsky, Margo.
  But a passage in wilderness / Margo Berdeshevsky.
    p. cm.
  ISBN 1-931357-50-1 (acid-free paper)
  I. Title.

PS3602.E7514B88 2007
811'.6--dc22

—Out of the wilderness of possibility

comes a vine without a name—

—William Stafford

But a Passage in Wilderness gives us poems of high-wire discovery. Sure-footed and tentative, Margo Berdeshevsky carries out a series of balancing acts. Nothing is preconceived, nothing is extraneous to her longing centering.

Her vision is lively and intensely contemporary. Wild coasts and urban streets, the homeless and the well-housed live in her images. In touch with what matters, on purpose, she goes frankly where she wants, willy-nilly, to be. She moves out into the world to see for herself and to do what she can.

Her themes are as wide-ranging as her geography. New York, Hawaii, Paris, Sumatra, cities and woodlands, petals and bones, winter, terror, joy, desire and de-lectation, infancy and age, luxury and poverty have all come home to her through experience, and find expression in her poems.

What makes *But a Passage in Wilderness* a unity, a big book and a small cosmos, is the depth of feeling it conveys, abundant and interactive, embodied and sen-sual. The poems are unfailingly fluent with emotional understanding, accurately invoked. A faithful dailyness radiates her words, even in her most daring flights. "Mother-ground," she says, "show me roots in your bare dirty kiss." She has taken her store of our language to heart.

When the earth quaked and the fatal tsunami struck the ground it stripped, Berdeshevsky went to Sumatra. Among the disasters of the aftermath, she worked for dear life and restoration, volunteering in a survivors' clinic. Grief and shocked lament also call for elegy and prophecy, she found—what Elaine Scarry calls "a life-saving reciprocity." Where everything seems lost, day begins again anyway, as Berdeshevsky's remarkable poem, "Brewing Tea," concludes:

There is harm. There is harm. I know the souls who mock all prayer, its invention. Its terrible optimism. And I know one old woman who knows only miracles. Only sight for

the blind, steps for the lame. When she dies I want her pillow to sleep on while the wind and the faithless converse with locusts. I want her lullaby, while I am forced longer at the

fire and at the daily storm, its useless windows cracking glass. The windhover, that priest, knew. Everything is a miracle, unseen. Brew the tea.

The power that causes tragic vision to flash forth from the juncture, in the stricken landscape, of the old woman and the pot of tea is, I think, one of the primitive powers of poetry. Berdeshevsky exercises it, with speed and great emotional plangency. It is the strategy of the active contemplative.

Her manner of making is not ancient or modern or postmodern but poetic. Her nonce forms are shaped by thought, for the particular occasion. She prefers a long overall form of developing meaning, carried out, related, with verbal tunefulness. She often chooses to unleash a long line and to keep it variable. Internal breath-breaks—not programmed—make these poems satisfying to read out loud or to read slowly, for the savor. Her effects are cumulative. Reading one poem sharpens the reading of the next, quite different poem. It assures the continuous ambiance of feeling that sustains her ideas.

Here is a poem, a short one, which nonetheless exhibits the level of intertextual aliveness that she achieves:

How to Open the Arms

I have been told. And in the returning bright
ahead of April I will carve a bird from a remnant bone, crone-
whisper it to fly, to be an owl, if it dares, haunt these passages,
what stolen heart and fresh blood in its delicate clasp,
arms, wide open?
The Filipina midwife who tells me how it is,
who watches lives coming in because I
crawl womb-ward, backward, busy
in my cave whittling bones of hope because,
always homesick for a tribe I do not, never
know how to join, like tracing paper—what
is a scream and what is a war, and what is
a hand for, if not for touching, making, what
is a wing for when it breaks, how to lie in kindness
how to plant for spring and not explosion's terrible
art—because, I make the infant lines, rather, have
a midwife to tell me how she mourns the deformed
baby girl, the blonde mother of three, dying stubbornly,
the metal marriage without love, the pale animals
all in one village who leave the land in concert,
on the wing.

Each phrase is responsive to the rest of the work it lives in. Thanks to her out-looking attention to events, her perceptions are immediate and persistent, and authenticate her "whittling bones of hope," even in times as hard as ours. The pulse of this poem is strongly marked. It rises from thoughts of self as a maker, self as lessoned by bird, then makes a central dive to where the self (rueful as earth and water fail) struggles to take in the examined moment, which then becomes a springboard toward the unity of the rescuing air. Operative words recur, propelling the three phases: because, because, because; how, how, how; what, what, what. They carry that pulse of feeling through the poem's three turns: rising, dropping back, and again rising. The midwife's grievous final list, taken in, yields a believable unsentimental hope.

The power to evoke credible grief and credible hope in great variety is paradigmatic in *But a Passage in Wilderness*. Her lines of elation are not free of knowledge of suffering, just as her lines of suffering are not free of knowledge of elation. It recalls William Blake's realistic, practical wisdom: "Without contraries there is no progression." Some such spirit animates Berdeshevsky's embrace of the real world. She moves us toward achieving balance, by exploring the co-existence of opposites and refusing to cast out any part of experience.

Her poems are never doing nothing. Her presence is vivid. She's a soloist, on her own, a world citizen at large in the new century. And in the same breath she is performing a profoundly social act. In making her lyric way, she takes her share of our language to heart, and gives it to us.

Marie Ponsot
New York City, August 2007

Contents

On Frailty

LONG DRUM

Long drum rolling peach
branch : *linaria cymbalaria*
: Mother of thousands.
Tongue-tied in adoration
I'll kneel to you who have
been losing faith like laundry,
all slow thrummed hours of it.
it
is the basket of fallen.
it
is that heroism I have remembered
to hate.   it,
falling fingernails and eager bees,
giddy already with one single day
call it spring, and
it is uncertain, pink.
Latin, or lacking
any language,
how this new air dresses up with
its dried elegiac tears. No more
winter. No more Septembers.
It reappears. Reinvents. Grows
a desert.
And there is, of course, a tree
rising. I who want to trust in it.
Each rare petal.

THE GEESE ARE BACK

i

The geese are back and
cherry-blossomed fists, raised;
Paris aches days before and beyond Good
Friday—nipple high in ochre, river so
full it hurts to be empty at any window.

When a woman sounds the deep-note scalpel as if
in a left-lobe fold, bone
flesh-bone flesh-bone the
cadaver soul says
yes, and hisses like her devil, birthing: Listen, risk: let's have it.

Know why I daren't, didn't I ever have or lose that
humanly? never
been beauty as April? Have I been a half-way
human cat hung upside-out since I was

Never day when it was night, never hot blown sand,
what is more—glass
than when the note is yes with
shards, one strain
trembles, a freezing songbird, then, all the geese—ever,
expiring.

Her voice
is a razor at its own tight throat, still
sings, still quavers a year after her worst
death. and I want that?
do I?

viol note that low, that just about to shatter
into bird but that real, a deep nerve, breaking:
real, make it real,
don't cry, make us feel, exorcise our—
we who are the dead love world, and we want to—
do I want that?
Agonies have this sound. Geese. And widows.

ii

Break a window at the skin, listen
cold,
as if it were before, speak
what risks, what matters. Why is it always death or birth, say
I come back, the geese could be wild violets, could bring breath from
Maroc—want that?
Do I flesh-boneflail my soul the same as
laugh? It cracks, once
in a while, and rarely into laugh, too;
there are women who can teach me, when I'm so weary of monsters,
and all magicians.

I always knelt for them, I always: preach me, teach me, love
me because
I am empty, humble, wide
open, I cry.

The Easter-
cross rotted this year from too much rain, flooding yellow
landscapes.
Who'll be love, what silver-bearded specter, or too old for me but eager
new or skin of every season opened—wound, grave with granite, will his
touch

tremble? Would I settle for hot breath and
intellect? I wanted
April. A poet.

Want: a red python standing on her wide, wet,
uncoiled, warning;
teaching there are others, all night hidden
constrictors, eager, well I want it,
like a leaf, like a tiny lime-colored new
thing, seen, the utter first; want it
crowning, whispering with straight talk; with smart; with correction.
Want: April. Change me, and do not be a magician.

Want it when the low note pierces inside me
too, knife-spear of
re-invent by scream, by poetry—
deep I could kill, deep dare deeper cry
my damaged dry-goods groan to be
more woman, less paper,
clothed as a more flesh beheaded sun exploding cat,
here, horizon, climb me.

iii

Daybreak, with the risk of loving, listen,
if the poem that shoots the heartbeat
bad as war,
on all that is middle—I know it hurts, but brave makes this
armor bow—
here is my
skeleton, hold it.

iv

If I pretend to invent nerves,
break me, each bone, each irritated wing.
Once I heard a woman say she longed only to see the far Pacific albatross.
She climbed where they—and then when her back was broken but she had seen,
she slipped and she fell, she
did not hate birds, or cliffs made for better claws.
She waited to heal, seeing rare beaks pale as the surgeon's mask
hovering, in the sheer
dark. Here's a human, here,
terror, I could never open again,
love, hear the high note, Beethoven, hearing—
Saint Francesco, not blind—
Not equal to one widow's howl? engine
of a human in the French afternoon; tin-
painted rain, rinse me.

v

These trees stand hurt with pink so laden still with girlhood
grace, I stumble.
Who would pardon beauty, now,
for furthering a woman at her double window,
face to Notre Dame, what secrets must women keep,
all women?

Blossoms are a short-story gasp, my twilight,
well penned as all a bookshop's hard covers.
I've returned to a second landing, shut one novel, read
divided glass, its late nacreous light like a winter crypt;
memorized the bursting pink-nailed fists below,
their open armed branches still the river current.

Branches, hold this: hold
the vagrant, for an hour;
dervish-dance without a wind, stop
weeping, woman; this is the butcher's street, and Paris.

vi

Go to the sea-bed for
days and days, see the old Micheline, the
baby gull throats yell
for music; march a wet and brown cold tide in
boots all caked with obsessive love,
oh sleep, how long, in her attic.
Eat the bottle-glass green,
the purple, like sea-aborted bloodweeds, with the eyes;
the soul on holiday from God.
I need an Easter fracture, from being. Need
violets genuflecting to anemones, her uncurled penis peonies,
her tulips tended by an old lady still and ever virgin
wet and ninety,
her garden of long French mornings.

She laughs, all of the time.
At home I have begun to read Spinoza.
Teach me what growing up for-ever has not:
how to temper molten with salt
water, how to be active as a god, or nature in April
hail.
I am not Mariner, nor ever meant to be.

In Possibility

Nighthawk, beetle, how do you pray? Is
landscape your good silence, your breviary?
Lilac, forsythia, honeysuckle, which of your
explosions on the branch of equinox with its passion
is the first to bite back at spring's dark nipple?
Nor your color on the palette, nor your love thrust
at all the suspicious landscape is tame: then what
beast, malcontent of her dungeon does not long for
dragon wings and muscle, put to use and gallop?
None.
The pagan's skirts are lifted. The vernal nest
built in every bare and upper tier, patient
with winter, and grief, lifts its chilled eye as well.
—Schubert-singer, ready for that first high G
of "Ave Maria." Light, waiting, well-trained yogi
holding breath long, long beyond our endurance,
—oh, for what strengthening? —Then let the ancient
games begin. Bring us leaps, gardens, and ripening,
this time of many grievings. Let the protector of truth come
down from her mythic hill, battered cloche and staff to
pierce the ground so swollen with story. Let the rose beetle
invent a loving. Claws in evidence. But kind. But possible.

BREWING TEA

In this dream, am no *she* created before Eve, no thief of men's seed or trance, no stalker,
no bad woman, no hungry woman, no seducer, no sad person, no bored mare in her vale,

no man. I see. And before these steps, all and as far as an eye can hold is charred
and remnant of, is desert where a green Hawaiian land was, is dark where light rippled.

Is utter with what has burned and galed and chilled and what is left: a petrified forest of,
a tortured shape, was another shape, before. Am seer, and walking. Is there one

complete and old and untouched stained house there, red wooden with thin banister,
thin porch? On a swing is the old, is the Johnny of the vale who died long ago who would

pray for me. In it are women with no names who welcome me as old beloved, I know
their eyes. In this distance of a valley shattered, that old man shuffles in like an actor, on

cue, and I am blessed and prayed for: my storm, my seeing. Dreamed into sitting down
in an ill lit room, its round table, to white bread, sour jam, and bitter tea.

No one will mention the blackened land, it is dark and dry, and that they are blind, and we
—are blind. We are in a complete house, standing wooden house that did not burn. All

day the gale dream returns, as though these remnants do not want me to forget them: red
house, its shuffle, its ghosts, its dregs who want me—to be seen. Am seer. I see. It was

a different day—where country stopped—there were houses with the sleeping bodies
curled within them. It was an island town on a razor's rim—the hour before

light's hour—empty, and arms wide with none and nothing to hold but sleep, the very
quiet storm. I see. Outside that town was one road to shoreline, there the patient men

22

with poles, long lines, and some with nets, held flash-lights to volcanic reefs. Blue fins, and parrotfish. There was no moon, and no cock had divided light from night yet.

When it did, I would be mountainside, above, watching like a fisherman, for ancestors, and wind. Like a roused sea, a descending flock of wings would come, their music must

be locusts, what other storm, what else would speak so biblically? I know men of little faith and women who lose their girlhood trust in that parent god who has no harm in his heart.

There is harm. There is harm. I know the souls who mock all prayer, its invention. Its terrible optimism. And I know one old woman who knows only miracles. Only sight for

the blind, steps for the lame. When she dies I want her pillow to sleep on while the wind and the faithless converse with locusts. I want her lullaby, while I am forced longer at the

fire and at the daily storm, its useless windows cracking glass. *The windhover*, that priest, knew. Everything is a miracle, unseen. Brew the tea.

i

Constellation-me, in the midnight where I belong.
In the velour waiting, our impermanence.
You say there are five security zones.
I need. I need. I need. One.

In the glare of my time, in the mauve aftermaths.
Afraid as I, what can I give?
Afraid of you, afraid as you: when we have lost everything, truly,
not only the village, not only the child, not only the notebook, not only the faith:

: a speaker calling the faithful to bow.
: a child in your lap demanding   Do you believe
in our god?
: a beetle, rebuilding her home in the mound.

Sun, always insisting: day. frailty. begin.

ii

Beware, oh my bewildered shark, and am I and am I no hunter, at all: the dark sun.
The zephyr of a more primitive wind, some Pierian spring, conferring thirst on she who
drinks, there, the dark sun. How frail the boat. We are crusty animals but—
the ark looks insufficient.

On the boat, will we be always thirsty? will we be cared for? will we be loved? will we be
saved. Ask.

Beware oh my Philomel who is not mine, but the sky's,

(am I and am I

tongue-cut and no

nightingale at all?)

Bewildered, I want to conjure in advance—of what we know,

poised, like Nijinsky.

And when, precisely do you imagine all this will take place? Because
    everything.

Breakage   poised.

HOW TO OPEN THE ARMS

I have been told. And in the returning bright
ahead of April I will carve a bird from a remnant bone, crone-
whisper it to fly, to be an owl, if it dares, haunt these passages,
what stolen heart and fresh blood in its delicate clasp,
arms, wide open?
The Filipina midwife who tells me how it is,
who watches lives coming in because I
crawl womb-ward, backward, busy
in my cave whittling bones of hope because,
always homesick for a tribe I do not, never
know how to join, like tracing paper—what
is a scream and what is a war, and what is
a hand for, if not for touching, making, what
is a wing for when it breaks, how to lie in kindness
how to plant for spring and not explosion's terrible
art—because, I make the infant lines, rather, have
a midwife to tell me how she mourns the deformed
baby girl, the blonde mother of three, dying stubbornly,
the metal marriage without love, the pale animals
all in one village who leave the land in concert,
on the wing.

Amber is a Tree's Blood

O slow soul, no desultory walk, now, but you vault in the spin of knowing, how
close how very near the end or the broken shell of this beginning you are.

How will I have used the amber hour, this is all I need like blood, to know. They
speak of fathers, well, I have buried mine in several mounds, in the sound of please

and thank you, in the lost bells of generation, silent in Moscow, silent in Prague, silent
in Paris, well I have buried mine in the breasts of men I begged, honor a crying girl,

she needs a home at any cost. Loss, or a dignified coverlet? Well I have buried mine in
a place where they forgot to engrave his name, and I said "sorry," for being the forgetful

one, O, Father, I wear your name etched in the moist of my unmarried mouth, Father,
will that do? Well, or do you require granite? We have spoken of forgiveness, touched

its chill Piscean body, teaming with the maggots of small minutes remembered. Days,
and years, are easier to grant an amnesty of maturity. Well am I mature, at fifty?

No desultory walk, now, no, go directly to the fire dust, place this body of a child with-
in a wheel within a wheel—child, with no child to honor but the hour. Well, brass

bell, cry, as gold. Bold-step to one tree that bleeds amber, for all that will be, a little
later. Sate the heart with such a father, rooted, in earth that cools this fever a little.

Mother-ground, show me roots, in your bare, dirty, kiss.

How he beat the dead woman, wife of wives. Dancer of slow-hipped dances, mother of mothers. How he kissed her womb of wombs. I'm coming in, he told the woman whose womb was dying ahead of the heart. And they made the dark island of love, one more time. How he rose on his knees on her bed and shouted: my wife. God, my wife. In one house, his father was ending slowly, in this house, a wife. His father went first. They saw the spirit lift. Each brother wore one of daddy's wide brim hats: the corpse thus honored, the good brothers cried. His mother was quiet. No more drinking and no more bruising. She kissed the old husband's brow and sat down.

When the wife died, they had moved her to the mother's house. There: the bed where daddy was. There: the wife of wives. In the tropic heat the Pleiades moved in its middle night. He stood outside their kitchen step and spoke to every ancestor in turn: The stars are the bones of our ancestors: his daddy had taught him. The wide brim hats rested on nails in the kitchen hall. His wife joined the October night. He saw her spirit, how it lifted out of her and up. Then like a hurricane he beat what was left until it looked as badly as he felt. The funeral was holy. Everyone prayed. And the box was closed, and his little boy and his smaller girl held his soft red hands that could build and bury. Most All Saints' Eves, October thirty-first for twenty autumns, he brought her flowers that danced for her in the Protestant Church yard where he touched her piece of earth as though it were that womb of wombs: I'm coming in. I'm coming in. This night—he told another woman: Yes I love you. Marry me. And she said no. I love you but I'm afraid. And the rain.

Born by Knife

Surgeon, when you opened the redhead's belly to deliver me,
did I look like I belonged? She taught me passages to mourn:
the good, the merciful, the meek, peace making.
When I never knew lava, its pulse, waiting. When I never knew
forsythia. When I never knew any changes as golden, as carriage.

I will learn again as if this mind had rooted with the last apples,
learn newly how to swallow the goodness of green, its boat,
its invented passages, the good, the merciful, the peace-making.
Open me, gods or killers of—does it need knives? Open my eyes
to the island of—tide of—unborn love, where I kneel
to a wide field. Be kind to me. I am returning. The dying
poet amongst us loses her way at birth.

Monet, thick secret of green weeds—a rowboat
with one oar, always ready. Oh, old man, going blind with color:
now, help me paint the water I am treading—help me bare tears
—like teeth, when my ankles are weakening. When love looks extinct.
Can I give up scripting history as though it were old flesh only
fire ants nest? Oh, bring me in, like clean wheat.

Unbreakable Umbilicus

There are six griefs in a room—its five persons, and time.
Time, unbreakable, time, unlineated,
scary business
of the heart.

In Claude Monet's thick secret of green
weeds, a rowboat with one oar, always ready.
There flies lean, like the old man
going blind with color. How I want to climb in. Old man,

old man, help me
to paint the water we're treading when
love looks extinct. History, as though it were
old flesh only fire ants nest.

Old reaper, bring us in, like clean wheat.
Help me to learn again as if this mind had
rooted with the last apples, how to swallow
the goodness of green, its boat.

Open me, gods, or killers of—
does it take knives?
Umbilicus to the unbreakable island of, tide of—
where I kneel to a wide field—

be kind to me, I am returning.
The oldest poet amongst us
loses her way at birth.

SPECIAL TALES IN TEN LINES

Rapunzel's hair goes gray. No horse riding a white knight—gallops.
Busy for a second coming, stung by wasps of dawn, sun will have bees in it.

Not milkwood or shine as mama's taffeta supper gown. In all of modern art
is there promise clean as the impressionist's window, or secret, as a room of

caged autumn? In a fairy tale are bluebeards, bears & dragons & villains &
swords, gold & power, frogs & cookies, spinning wheels, death, slippers. In

a life—that, & the repetitious yellow we cling to: mimosa. mimosa. mimosa.
I ask the blind, what is pretty? Stop counting the dust. Oh where is the gazelle's

thin ankled canter? Where, my coach of mice to tempt me? Poor bleeding little
mouse, us. And another, climbing, enraging the leg it mistakes for mother.

— 2 —

WHOM BEGGARS CALL

This Sentence

(does not seem to contain a main clause)

As though it interrupted the rain, this arabesque
kick of silver. Spun sand-veil, in the storm.
Its broken bodies
disjointed.
Light. As though the small across the dim—stopped
the road. Or as if shyness surrendered its torture, in order
to laugh. As though a war heard its name, and listened
to prayer. As
though last light would wait for my own entrance,
skirt hem dirty but so utterly available.

If light, used, as an old idea, fractured shard plunged in
as a murder undeserved and terrible. And told as often as
the death of Christ,   this is how it is, this is how it was.

If light crashed and I   walked in it, insistent,
if I entered and if it hurt.
And if the dark were no heroine with a tragic flaw,
nor strange.
As though a simple stop. Mere veil, to save it. Light,
I mean, broken, as a spine. Light, at the borders of
our sentence, living on the train of the gown
as we do, available   for lifting.
Here is what it has led to.

Whom Beggars Call

…and a heart that understands cuts like rust in the bones. —St. Augustine

The two at the church door say "*Ma fille,*" they know I need,
they French-style kiss my

"*bises,*"
from beggars,
kiss me, twice.

The man who cannot love me whom I
chews his   say I   cannot correct,   or love.

Like blue foxes, or birds,
graciously, the holy night
folds.

Or
Christmas stalks toward slouching Bethlehem again, the markets are ripe with foie gras,
and people will eat well   while my beggarbrave days,

Oh obviously I see the concentrated man beside the church wall, so near if he was animal,
he'd bite. He's drowning in plastic, and bottles, and bread, and blood. He's carefully
daubing at his forearms with white paper, seining scabs in the thin noon, this rain is
straight-pins, he's a serious kid inspecting his skinned knees in it, his arms bleed so near
if he was animal—

I pull my black woolen glove, I'll empty all my pockets to his un-expectant hand, no not
touching it. I watch my coins, how they slip his loose claw. It's because of how I have
purposely eluded making a skin contact, it's because his lips, his water-eyes, I know how
to drown, and I look in his glare, the red-rimmed lakes so near the River Seine, and my
voice says "*Go get something for the arms, your arms, yes?*"

"*Oui petite Madame, oui, c'est clair,*" in his sidewalk lair he looks in me all blear and limpid at the same, how is it possible, to correct? One hand shoots out at me to shake my hand—a gentleman. The heartbeat drowns me. Can I not touch the leper? Or, I take his skin to skin, cold off-key sweetness in it, hands like aftertastes of bitter almond, rinds, oh open walnuts. In the rain, my glove, my black woolen house is too bright already.

In a blizzard dawn in another house, a red haired son rolls to his mother's stretch-marked belly, speaks in sleep, "*You're all the light I'll ever need.*" On my worried stairs, I'm the glass one, sadder one, older one whom beggars still call "*little lady,*" and want to touch.

★

I am not wise.
I hide in churches.
The healer looks at me, and says I'm an exploded windshield, fissures sprayed across the feet of chance. She says the break unveils the fragile underbelly and that's good. A strength.
Fragile. Strength. Fragile. Strength or mumbling like a beggar's mantra, cross the Pont des Arts.

I let him go like death, uncorrected.
Or graciously, the holy night folds my heart and other pages I have tried to memorize, slowly as a blindness in its infant light.
Or
Christmas stalks toward slouching Bethlehem again, the markets ripe with
and the man
chews his own bones, blue fox in its winter snare. He bites his rosewood
pipe, or cannot love. Let's say I try to heal him. Let's say I try to heal him and I cannot, or, he needs to be corrected. Or, tended by mendicants, bells,
the terrible starved angels speak.

I stain it on the mirror's palette: *change!*   I scrawl it 'cross the marble, manic as that man of bones, or make it in a burned sienna lipstick-blood, beginning of a murderer's tale or scant salvation. *Change.* And Christmas stalks the hearts.

At the round dark vault that houses Mary Mother of

I light my mama's candle,

"here, dead bird,"

and mutter until I think I begin to fathom it: our mothers. our births. our begging.

If there were ways to get to sides of lakes of no circumference.

Or two beside the church-door pray,

"On fait la bise, ma fille?"

They want to kiss me for my coin. *"Que le bon Dieu t'aide, ce soir,*

ma fille. On fait la bise?" as though I may not say but Yes, and kiss me.

The man

chews his own bones like tough birds, like the fox, bites his pipe, or cannot

love. Let's say I try to heal him.

Say dragonfly, spine, convulsing. Say sad or manic or belly flayed toward what invented

him, or God why are my wings in your teeth? Say I pray, I correct, I pray. I pray for this

whole cold season, stair after stair, oh obsessed as a roof-rat, her nest of dark red sleeps,

the tangle of her unbrushed hair.

★

Well I'm an actress who knows only a few of her lines.

As close to Advent as to her cave, unable to dream; or   There is

a dream, I'm playing the mad Ophelia again. I'm humming snatches, broken-boned.

There's paper in my mouth, I'm eating a postcard from my lost love, chewing it, oh

absentmindedly   the words I have not read may get inside me this way   may leave

their inks on my mouth, stains— *"Oh where is the beauteous majesty of—"*   line-

plunged birdlings, of the rain.

I am haunted by the grim

man I am trying to heal.

Your tall and educated walls—Break them. Your fortune, lose it. Your everything, too big for you. Your all that is the wound, unhealed. I send you pieces of God with my shaking hands. Chew them, along with your bones. In dream I'll meet your demons, twice their size. How my hands are but salt, are raw with the daily sea. How I am haunted by giving up. By your elegant fire-pit, gone gray. Or Christmas stalks toward slouching Bethlehem again, the markets, ripe with foie gras, and the people will

Oh obviously I see the other, so near if he was animal, he'd bite. He's drowning in— He's carefully daubing at—inspecting knees in it, his arms bleed so if he was animal—he'd chew them off, or caught.

I pull my woolen empty, all my no—not touching it. It's because of how I have purposely, because of his lips, his water-eyes, I know how to drown. *"Your arms, yes?"* or Christmas stalks whom beggars call—

"Oui petite Madame, oui, c'est clair.
"Que le bon Dieu t'aide ce soir, ma fille,"
in his sidewalk blear
how is it possible,
to correct?

"I heal you with correction. You need to be corrected." Alice said so. I heard her.
One hand shoots out at me to shake my hand—a gentleman. The heartbeat drowns me, skin to skin, cold off-key sweetness in it, hands like aftertastes of bitter almond, rinds, oh open walnuts. *Change*, I scrawled across my mirror, before I left my dark house. *Change*, for a merry Christmas. In the rain, my glove, my black woolen house is too bright already.

In a blizzard dawn in another house, a red haired son rolls to his mother's stretch-marked belly, speaks in sleep, *"You're all the light I'll ever need."* On my worried stairs, I'm the glass one, see-through one, or older one whom beggars still call "little lady," and want to touch.

["I heal you with correction, you need to be corrected." —Alice Notley]

38

WALKING PAPERS

There are fifteen blind, in matched olive green shirts and rubber
soles crossing la Rue de Rivoli in sun too bright for naked lenses.
Each one's right hand holds the shoulder of one ahead, moving
mass of adaptation, the first one, no shoulder bone to dig her fingers
into reaches hers—out thrust, in not fear and not confident, there is
no one ahead of her—but airborne fine seekers of, forward in motions.
They are a single bonded sensor. Are dependent on noise and breath.
When traffic parts like a lava wash—sparing one holy relative of
a goddess' hut, I want to place my own hand on the last shoulder, walk
in darkness, that way, conjoined by seeking, matched in some way
green as earthen things, and touching. Landing on the shaded side
of the boulevard none will drop the chain to wipe a sweat salting her
endless eyes. Frightened by the day we have in front of our hands,
nailed nerves dry tears to the whites of seeing.

In Progress

i

———————————————

Come to Lisieux, one says.
That town where they make lace?
yes.
That town where Thérèse saw her own
hands bleed?
yes.
A lace of recent sorrow?
no. it was not there.
Lace makers and their bobbins.
ah. yes.
Fields nearby. Golden hay rounds.
yes.
Vultures?
no, not here.
Go alone on your borrowed bicycle, laughing.
Are there crows?
crying.

And at the claws of a chateau, shadows cupping
poppies so bright they hurt a heart with happiness.
yes. bright as sunsets, beheaded.

Crying?
if you must.
Riding alone?
well, crows dance together. and
vultures smell of roadkill, invade

the pine-trees so suddenly, one says.
But not with my owls.
not with my midnight wings. no.

Owls.
Dead Cassandra was like an owl, one says.
serpent tongues hidden in her ears. Unbelieved.
yes. and sacrificed and raped in a temple. yes.

Come to Lisieux, little Saint Thérèse is here,
stigmata in her palms while her father
watched.
yes. but there are also gardens, of lace.

In the Egyptian book of the dead, one says
I am the crocodile god who dwelleth amid
the dead men's terrors.

And *les hiboux* conduct souls, they say.
yes. in Lisieux, let's buy beautiful lace.

ii

An owl conducts souls, they say.
yes but terrifying too,
an owl can devour its own mother, they say,
could kill the father, such a child. Cries a
gray shawled sound, lace, in the heat.

Summer solstice is the day of the owl,
one says. But vultures are more frightening.
yes.

iii

In the Musée Pompidou's modern China room, a flock of white furred, winged, rabbits clamor for attention, their glassed little amber stares eyeing the time we have come to. Some are climbing on each other's spines, some are crouched but only on two legs, now, they are birds, see, their artisan sculptor has invented a new race, duck-winged and owlish out of rabbits—what could he do with us?—this new creature, who will invent?

We stare all afternoon at that sculpted installation of winged and furred who nearly look like owls, but no they're not, read the title, it says that he has sewn on downed white duck wings, tucked their little chests and bellies, made them into no owls we really know, but displaced as, or homeless hunters as

oh,
to be drunk on the holy,
on the holy spirit,
on the owl,
not afraid of any heat, not afraid of any day, or any night,
a soul conducted,
every portrait, holy,

our joyous

alone on a bicycle that does not belong to anyone,

let's, please, buy beautiful lace.

on the hottest day, our globe all out of control, as usual,

ignore a moon, its skin-veiled skull,

an angel may be watching such progress, my darling.

BUT A PASSAGE IN WILDERNESS

i

But a woman prepares to cross the perfumed
river, little crying.

She has left candles placed like birds with folded wings.
When they are lit, she will watch their heartbeats burn.

Sings,
night-sphinx of rivers, am I eye to eye with your light,
or closer to your claw,   tell me this.

Sings the thousand prayers like ponies vying with winners, how
they know the course, but cannot stretch their white-downed spines
to gallop, can't span the fathoms with kicked   light.

Broken-eyed roses, colts, don't fall!
Dark matter of the daily heart, do something beautiful.   Do this.

Between soul and stone, there is grass, its mere and pushing green.

Once, there was a wind heavy as a wilderness, made in its soul to
be without ground, and with song.   Incantation, magic, serenity,
each, so near.

ii

Do not abandon me. (Louise Bourgeois, at 90.)

43

iii

Here is an autumnal phrasing: Though all
the crimson windows of the season are symphonic,
only the viol's carousel can speak.

Now they veer toward bone, toward tin. These leaves. These
small red hands. But now they burn. Now they grow fine claws,
and spread them. Now they say Our Father, in every language
including silence. How they ask for one true sentence, and a
woman says it: "For sale: love, hardly used." She is no
Renaissance mystic.   Never meant to be.

Tell me. Tell me.

a.

that woman—that keeper of star-gates and wombs
wonders if angels are angered; that midwife
has things to tell me: every white animal in her village
died on "all souls' night," a day not venerated there.
all the white animals; the pure white parakeet, her
perfect-pale goldfish in his pond of darker carp.

if there is a colored cloth unraveling, threads hung from
heart-bones like those ripped cloths on jagged stones in
Lebanon where figs crack rocks to have their Jew
life, tell me.   come, hang your torn

cloths from my fingernails and say that my survival will heal
your humanity. come hang as fathers did from a Pogrom's
wild-pine limb, blue-lipped with history.
I want to hold your story like an egg.   tell me.

b.

a man who stained the sidewalk with white paint until it held
him in its black clasp. the paint remains.

c.

a tiny tongue, star-shower-bright with desire, mewling for flight.
so tempted. what makes your small lung rattle with longing?
you do not know the taste, have never swallowed blood, all
your genetics clock the music of bones fractured in your teeth.

45

the thrill of leaping.   tell me.   at the crossing bridge,
black satin-sheen below, a rail so simple, step would never
have been easier, a dying no unkinder than love.

the Tour Eiffel, the thin and vain Jean Cocteau's
prancing twin, so gorgeously, orgasmically, piping light.

d.
but   blinded/ guilty/ orphaned/ or crushed   or bound   but   witnessed/
or failed/ or foretold.

haunted   abandoned   missed   malformed   floral.

To be its mother.

Grief, what kind of a teacher are you?

EVERY AFTERNOON

Am not the precious thread of water or round
whispered pattern the spider prays and prays.
If I am not of greatness now not a russet overdue
pregnancy of a moon spreading birth across
the late sky and not love and not of eminence
not the first narrative or aria ever in the sound of days
or not the first and perfect green morning
then I am poor near all symphony, all love.

Am mere, and tempted with wind, and the visiting
plover. Am twisted with words remembered by
the old men, knitted by drifting women, am old
enough to have hand prints in my heart. History.
I am frightened of those who blame nothing.

If I am not art for change or known to a jungle
stone except I embrace it, animal, and clinging,
forgive my life,   it is alarmed to be no storm or epic
no astonishment to a migration of whales in their
sapphire winter no stanza hissed by a last born
messenger and repeated by the first
forgive my life it worries so, to thank, and hate,
for making me innocent of genius. It breaks
as earth created and not known
at the end of the day not dusk's earliest sun
but the long night's daughter. It breaks, every afternoon.

47

Of Days

If it were not for the perfume of the tropical lily,
to call death by her modern name is not glamorous.

Not Snow Queen, Freya, Hel or Santa Muerte,
not Oya's colored rags or Maman Brigitte's willow.

Now, sapphirine in the morning glories closes the
compline hour. As long as I could, which was all

day, I watched excellence, end of summer leaf gowns,
yellowing quietly as an attic wedding glove, its kiss.

Long as I could I was ashamed of comfort and silk sleep
while others floated face down and the ground swelled.

Long as I could I praised change and the ark,
some were always saved. Drowning and an unseen fist

of the beloved, saved. As long as I could I said bless and thank.
There were no blasts in this morning's apocalypse.

Only a crow lying down with her scorpion in the shade. She
would not change her story.

For Thanks

In one room old with darkness
are two who do not see until
some defending angel gives
him an old wives' trick, a daily
cucumber for breakfast, and he sees
that she is pretty; gives his beloved wife
a knife to open cataracts, and she
dances to bring two dozen eggs for thanks,
one born broken. Bring the foreigner rice,
she sings, and closes that eye that briefly
saw the room, the darkness, her husband
counting her curves with a candle,
and where her grand-child's umbilical cord
will be buried, at their step.
In defense, the angel breaks another egg.

HOLY AS A BIRD

—Dearest one—Are you in Paris now, and safe? Is anyplace on this globe safe? Everyone here is sad and scared. Please let me know where you are, how.   love.   as always.

Cliffs & ocean-turtles nod
where she is mouthing her terrible thanks,
her lips smeared with the stillpoint, call it Christ — He would.

———————————————

Everything that has to do with the soul's work is dangerous to happiness, is all that is left to do. The life stories are tangential. Ghosts & ancestors & earthworms. All I want to be is part of something. The soul is full of one who is dead and plays her piano; of one who makes babies; of one who mourns. We are so nude it frightens God.

———————————————

I swallow the body of love wherever I can, am cannibal, hungry as never before. I dream of owls, I hunt with them. My lips are smeared.   But if I can plant a hill of golden—if, render beauty to one awful branch—the idea is only holy, as a bird.

Heal us. The pale one looks at me, with my own gray-painted eyes. She tugs at my chain, she climbs me, ivory claws that break my breast-flesh when I lean, I can not remove her—she has landed from the warm wind and she is the soul's help. its kiss. its hand. You can't get rid of magic, she howls, you will need her, like milk, like freedom.

woman. cannibal. starved.

———————————————

You'll be born.   You're just mortally terrified, like every being half way out of the womb and into ice.   This is a face that cannot, will not. Bird of difficulty, too thin to battle all that rain, steals her pale page like a forged travel pass.   here, mama, make me.

She beats her feathery   against the all-hued high window,   how many bones   does she own?   Then she stops,   to mourn un-nameable songs, how many.

Let go, until the wild dog, his damp smell, makes you thirst and swallow dust. Let go until the black animal drags your heart through whitish eggs, their writhing hatchlings. Understanding   is no deal.   Let go until the thing is soiled and cursorily laundered. Let it hang in this chill new weather,   oil on every wing.

When you announce principles of the spirit, you will die for them, that is the deal. Fingernails will be unclean, even your dead mother would see that. You'll say yes but look they are dirty with soul-blood, I have been working! see? Your mama's ghost will sashay to the cobalt sea, will disappear; she always comes around, at this cold, daring hour at the end of another year.   She does not want a cross on her forehead.

The hand cringes.   The hand is the soul, is all over my walls.   It acts.   Is the activator.   Handprints, like pale owls, hover.   Born. You'll be born outside. Bald fists of the linden trees shoot up like fat, ferocious dancers, to fight back.   Is this the moment to fight back?   It will not speak, it is sky,   it does not have to.

You'll be born anyway, and backwards.   Though the cranes are crossing all the skies of France and they are bleeding. How they dangle their thin limbs, undressing. The soul will be left, will cry like the last and only sound a rabbit makes, or like an annunciation. Nobody gets to the belly of God   standing. That is a given. And you hate it.

Cut, and cut, and cut away the stone.

Here, hummingbirds must
halt at my window.
How in the dark, in the meditative hour
blindness comes—a bell
around this need—a she who used to be
beloved by mirrors—what harbor shelters
peace, she dares to not scream.
She wants an angel she can smell, she yells.
All paradise answers with its shrug.
And a boy in a treetop, going blind.

Isn't this the moment to recall walking on hot coals surrounded by quiet guards, call them
angels.   He would.   silver, with their obedient concern.

But, "Sister, speak to me of love," the bird says — that the almond tree might blossom.

★

− 3 −

THE STORY

Lautrec, I've Heard, Shot Spiders

I'm told Vietnamese will not kill a spider, that tiny ones escape the body when it sleeps, as bones, in deconstructed dream. I read Toulouse Lautrec, weary of being small, spent the hot French afternoon shooting at a spinner inside her threads. His crippled little legs, crossed as the beast's thin star. My cat arches at his proud murder. Stop killing that rice-bird, I shout, the way I want to shout at my country. What butterfly does not know she dips and bows for the opera's fifth act?

Without legs, the smooth stones are standing, the surinam cherries cape earth beneath them; at my door, their bitter bright. And each day's complex webs uphold a star as grass holds on to fragmentation, unable anymore to bear burdens. Who speaks the nightingale's creativity, notes that never were, before they are?

Then is there one casual, unimportant death? Words that owe the lenders flesh, and nothing more—On the final day, or on the first—how are you really? Sometimes I do not speak for days. Can none but the inventive nightingale know balance?

Chameleonic love, or hate, springs branch to branch, toes splayed, flame tongued, and spitting. Spitting. And that tiny heart. Then, artist, color us—on our knees, to please some God we used to believe in. I try to sing a color, pretend I am that nightingale, fail, all summer long.

Wrap, then, the wounded whom you know of and dare not forget. That is not all you can give to the end of civilization if that is what today is. But that is the daily, and the daily, and the daily. I wish to baptize a bird. This, the season of explosions. How can you promise to believe? Trust in the surinam fruit, that its juice will be bitter. Trust daylight to tread water. The dragonfly is not drowning. Ever since the earliest wanderer grew birdness, the palm of the breadfruit has been opening.

LATE

under ferns, their wide coiled lace embrace
in decadence and green, their luxury of curling
like another animal—late, there is light, coiled.
The lizard does this too, the one blue one jade-
eyed male cat. Ferns, in shade and dapple. Shadow
shaping thread between all emerald thumbs and octaves
—to all its other hands.

This is the love of a jungle, its unlatched gate. This is retreat
from a war, a porch where the life of the land is a true thing
or all that is right is breeze. A king of the skies in limbic flight,
a parenthesis of black, way up there. He forecasts rain that will
not fall yet. But it will. What is right is the impossibility
of numbering variants of green. Stick-figure dignities
of sugarcane. Dancers, bending only cursorily, to be
polite. Their fields of bare, reserved curves, wiggling.

Under the candle leaves, taller, more complex, more
tree—this year than when they took early white root—
it is possible to imitate their curl, their un-furl. To open
from one position to its kin. To participate in change
without despair. Grateful for dozing and the dove's
wakeful, pearled coo.

One hour—knows the heavy tongue of peace. Wind,
in waiting. How its thighs will open, to be entered.

IMPLIED AS ADIEU

There is no war, here.
White milk-soft bodies of the Koi fish
loop our pools, patrol unspeaking
romance, undulating. Poetry is more
important, this season. Solace, as a mist.
While Koi bellies—in repeated symphony,
collective as the flies, but so much prettier—
There is no war, here.
Voice, as pebble in between the sheer and the dangerous.
Granite, and a mica of repetitions meant for hope.
Unreasonable delicacy. No war. So lace a rain, it breaks.
On one leg, we are as pelicans. Angling for finesse.
Catching peace on a nervous string.
Sun is gone and the Koi at their Sysiphan orgy—
are a pond of sperm, unspilled. Implied
as adieu. There is no war, here.
There is no war, here. Only lace,
under the skin. Oblivious
fish at the round bridge, touching
each others' nests of pale bullets.
Your holding—is woven as the jungle.
My soul at the painted bridge wants
your uncontrolled hand.
You, too Zen to kiss with all your mind.
We break, every afternoon.

THE STORY

To learn how to die, watch cherry blossoms, observe chrysanthemums. —Anonymous, 1700

While the horned cow tethered in her yard is walked to a shoveled pit,
her throat slit for a week's meat, blood hissing in what the knife has opened
for that song—the village boys applaud—

The wind has no passport, knows no border, nor a sky that is not land.
The sea knows not its border either, hungry as a village statue for
a fresh and red hibiscus dutifully placed, behind a carved stone ear.

Was it hunger, I ask. Awake and asleep in the silt nights, I try to float
in the sea of souls. But that is not a comfort. Water is for washing away
a tropic sweat at the equator's fence, but the sea?

This is the story: It is noon. A man grabs his wife—drops
everything, takes nothing.   Come.   And he guns their jeep only
inches ahead of the second and the third and fourth black wave-walls
rising—the slower car behind them lost, in greedy water.

The man knows he must turn right, up the next tight road and grab his
mother, save his mother. A bag-of-bones old woman hobble-canes in
front of him, bent, and slowing his escape, his engine seething, he
jumps out, grasps her body, throws her in back of his mother-bound jeep
and guns right. Not that way, go left, the woman storms. But no—my
mother—Your mother will be all right, turn left, turn left up this hill
she screams, or you will die.

By then the desperate ones cling to his car and shout Left, Go left, Go
up. Surrounded, he succumbs. And turns. While water behind his spine
swells blood and floods—It drowns all that is to the right. And he drives
higher, to the highest point the road will carry. There, the old woman

clambers out and vanishes. And there is his mother, already on high
ground, and all in her street where he had wanted to go, gone with
the ravenous Indian sea that could be any ocean next, suppose.

Every year is the most terrible. A sun. A red breeze. A humming teen-
boy's favorite music in the tongue of the most powerful voices on the earth,
at his pillow. Near a window, near another tethered cow, near a wide-hipped
moon. Any wave is the sea of souls. Any soul its captive beloved.

—Sumatra tsunami, December 26, 2004—

After the End After the Beginning

Tears in the eyes of fishes—Basho

After the end of the world, the dragon flies are the first,
returning. Frogs in chorus in a lead-weight rain, the bones
of buffalo, pissing.

After the end of the world, a shredded page, uprooted
monster trees. A blue jacket, a lace head cloth, a black
boot on a wheelchair stem, a mudded page of the floating
Koran.

After the end of the world, flooded rice fields, a blind
child seeing ghosts of ghosts, stabs his forefingers in his
eyes, screaming.

After the end of the world, Ayesha is chopping chiles to
spice our gruel—I was crazy but now I sing for the world,
she says and says and says again. After the end of the world,
a crazy woman who loves God, singing ahead of the heat.
After the end of the world, a woman who sings that the bad
ones perished,   Allehu   Akbar   in the next hot dawn again
and again, ever after.

After the end of the world, over and over—I lost, I lost, I lost,
and God is great, the mosquito ballet meeting the dragon flies,
circling.

This is not a dream, this is a tragedy, a boy making his words
a sing-song, spindle-shins, kicking. After red words on the broken
columns: this is not a dream, this was tragedy, fresh fish who may
have wedding rings in their bellies.

59

After the end, a new market. After the end, what kind of town had
it been?   yellow velvet, and minarets.   a shredded boot.   blue
china, broken.   a baby's rubber thong, not screaming.

After the finale, smiles left that say, I lived.   I dream of
corpses drowned in the noonday heat. What time is it now?

After the end of the world, the taro plant blooms in another
language, its flood-root, fetid emerald in the mud. After the end
of the world   bruised   dirty   determined Sisyphus—who
ever breathes—rebuilds.

—Aceh, December 26, 2004—

The Vehicle

i

The living call across the wriggling, readjusting
sonofabitch sea to say: we were afraid again.
the dogs who howled themselves to sleep
are still again. The earth quake came again, last
night, dividing sea with its teeth and visiting
death-touch to another thousand. A different island.
On this one, lime-green afternoon and cloud-touch,
shadow like a light cologne. A squall across this rest
above a rice field, its egrets. It came in the dark,
this time,
that's what the living say, who outlived Christ's
last
holy day. Now this one.

ii

When I knew a dying man and when his
fingernails were turning blue, acceptance
he said, enlightenment is the acceptance
of the unacceptable.

How our histories
have tried to remember,   to reward,   to reason,

our stories brimming with what is fought and
fought against,   and sometimes a little lace,
a little dark wine,   a little heartbeat.

Feel this, she showed me: putting my finger on
the pulse in an umbilical cord not yet
cut between the infant and its birth-sac—the
second, born.

Hold this, she asked: a flashlight, so she could sew a
torn mouth where the birth had been.

And both of us knew the man I speak of. Who never left
you without saying this: drive carefully.

—Sumatra, 2005—

CAIN—AFTER

Buried himself. Cried.

Like a departing wind amid the palms,
rattling: the quiet of no more God,

And no more flesh-between-his-fists brother,

And no more first green breath shooting up with
—you have tilled me, made me—
—never—

The boy-made-man stood severed—
mark—on his inner eye that would be heart, hereafter.

God, he whispered—You—
I—who never killed,   but pulled a root from the good
brown soil—learned from You who loved blood,   better.

He didn't believe it.
Looked at his large hands that had held
the little brother's throat, like a tiny bird.

Hands that had scraped black stones, and planted,
and were forbidden, now: No planting.

He was tired. Rubbed his eyes like a littler boy.
Knelt.

Used those hands to scrape a bed in the earth,
under the billion stars   coming out:
—eyes of God—
Who would never.

Lay in his bed he'd made. Never slept. Not now.
Not ever.
God damn.

Equinox Africa

In tones of metal rectangle, like an empty corridor,
the girl, an inch off center, thirty inches tall—her toes
turned inward as a stopped bird—trails her ragged cape
of used dry leaves. It hangs from sparrow bones, drapes
the shoulders loose with ungrown hinges, certainly not
wings. Only her large brown shoes are sturdy.

And, here are stones,
softened to inedible lentils.

What colors memory, with its emotive
fuchsia? cognitive as hell you'd say if
you were a skull at a war trial. Brittle.
But if we swore like trilling hills,
tongues, torn loose, and we were less the
dead, more swirling hips and ribs and heels,
standing on the moon's deep rebellions.
No. We tried that.

The year's new peach branch celebrates certainty,
instead of that despairing that the day provides,
and a first forsythia forbids, dearest.

We try that.
when crows demand a daylight and repeat it with
iridescent authority, shined as stars.
We try that,

when the length of day and night are
approximately equal everywhere on earth,

or

she turns her face not quite to us,
not quite to the bald
white skulls laid like ordered seashells as wide an angle
as any shore of civilization. there can be no harsher eye
on dirt. this was my church. what was ours.

Un–titled

– a collage with words that won't stop the nonexistent trains that words keep coming –

No saints of light like Lucy with her dish of eyes.

Not blind, laying wrapped in flags and shrouds   but
slaves & fancy dancers speaking the tune to water—
waters not having stopped with waves—bearing
not having paused with breaking.

The poor had no busses, the poor had no trains,
no chariot to wind them on home.   Night-eyed now,
quiet Orleans laying down her Elysium,   shiny
blow horns muted under winds that came and did
what prophets said they would: kill.   rains that did
what seers said they would: flood, come the bright.

The bus named want—that Blanche called Desire,
now water-ghost tired in wet that keeps on washing up,
how small our hands that never may come clean,   (only)
little ghost Cordelia comes: babbling like another lost
chile' to her homeless Lear:
              All blest secrets,
All you unpublished virtues of the earth,
Spring with my tears! be aidant and remediate
In the good man's distress! Seek, seek for him
Lest his ungoverned rage dissolve the life
That wants the means to lead it.

The poor had no busses. the poor had no trains.
coming to carry them home.
In America, it's labor day, saints, like
live rodents,   swimming & training.
Not beggars, with dishes of vision.

—Hurricane Katrina, 2005—

To Autumn

A soldier chalks two words on New York sidewalks, no other hector in his hand.
They are "love" and "heals." Crowds gather, crowds soften like an herb
that's pounded into poultice for a shattered bone, to knit it. "Love heals"
remains. It rains.

——————————————

In the rain, and when the healers are gone who heals when they are gone
and who heals the gone in autumn, where is my bed and what is the work
of love, its dark attacks and rescues, poultices or words,   what work is
emptiness where peace was, how do you know that love heals   it
turns, in the earth   in the promise   in our air.

Without question marks we lie in the question. Its unmarked longing. No
rain erasing.

a. and   *b.* and   *c.*

——————————————

In zealot tides I dream of dead healers.
Kalua, in Lahaina. Empedocles, in Sicily.
This year of wars that have not died, no matter
how many healers. This mouth that spouts like birthing
whales in a poisoned sea, but wordless.

In a corner of the dream, in the corner is a dwarf old woman
curled up in fetus, she is stiff and iridescent flies are at her eyes,
you have to bury her.
I am asleep beside an island pine, its wide twined root,
this is where I shovel-break the dirt to make a bed for her,
soiled clothes,   felt hat,   flies.

I'll sleep where she slept now, on flat stones, near the wall,
she, in the softened earth. The healers are—I don't know where but gone.
Is it time to speak of how it flowed from our hands for the calling
like falcons, come, please come,   is it time to speak of helping?

————————————————

Healing haunts my walls.
Are you a healer?

Sometimes.
If healers taught you,
what do you know?

a.   *b.*   *c.*

Am doe in car lamps, knees locked,

suspect there is a word for faith,
its truth, its trial, its wall.
I want there to be such a word.
To trust it. Suspect, they taught us trust.

a.   *b.*   *c.*

————————————————

For faith, I suspect its cell⠀⠀its mustard grain and mountain may
be lost. Suspect there is still love. And air, for the airless, promised.
a.⠀⠀⠀⠀*b.*⠀⠀⠀⠀*c.*

Trust me, I want to say,
I can wear blood like child soldiers do,
bright finger paint across our souls—

Autumn mother, mere challenger—I can close your eye.

I give you my on-fire palms.

Trust me I can hold your terrible hand when you bleed and are afraid.
Trust when the God-name has become a sorrow.⠀⠀overused.⠀⠀vain.
Why, one asks.
Longing, I say.

Light, I say, come with my woman's welcome I have to offer.
We don't know what heals. But know the miracle that is loved
and gone. Spontaneous. And gone. Say come to this heat I have
and I can help you burn. I can help you paint. I can help you cry.

You cry in vain. When one fight's done, another crouches ready.
In the corner of a dream, the dwarf. In another, the lover like a giant.
Dying's in our bodies, as normal as a war and leaf fall. Normal as
longing.⠀⠀⠀⠀*a.* and⠀⠀*b.* and⠀⠀*c.*

In the Musée de la Vie Romantique are two framed locks of George
Sand's saved white hair, glassed gold, her gifts of tiny rings, ash pearls.
"I only care about things that come from the people I loved and who are
gone," she said. An autumn thorn is rooting in a black torrential rain where
she is gone and her love is gone, dour Chopin's piano haunting soft cloth
walls, as though it could not quiet.

Here is my hand, my hand because I have no more to give. Here my broken
art, for the same reason. Autumn mother, is there a wailing wall anywhere that
cannot answer your solemnity? We are being taught to cry.

Oh soft Autumn, come. I have no son for you.

★

In the Falling of Late Fire Days

when the church bells overcome
my mornings.
when the kiss ungiven
blinds my thighs.
while we are hungry,
for wombs,
or births,
or both.
I am the woman
asking.
all wombs.
all hearts.
all crying.
all receiving.
we are the women at our own temples,
tapping marble, as if it might be silk.
walls, as if a creviced message hid.
we enter.
as if born meant capture
of the hearts' torn milk-teeth, grinding.
when you have wept and sung psalms, too,
and high-noon is perfect with its ferocity
of autumn,
tear the hour, like a saw-toothed paper cat,
limb from limb,
and pray for peace.
or do you know another mantra,
mother?

Then let's not go to the Ganges again and die.
I will not need to remember, not weep
in quiet Terezin, that dim cry;
but if I could steal one of your lifetimes,
it would be a girl kneeling for Botticelli in the wind;
no, would be "the beloved," that ability,
just once, perfected. Why do some know how?
When swans of Prague arrive like verdigris
in old ice broken for April, come then
beside the amber filth that rivers there,
lose your way in her camellia coated fog,
hunt the castle ridge where hungry men meet;
be uncertain; but meet me there. You will not die
beside the Vltava. This is the only promise
one may make, this year.

We'll kneel to a park–bench–druid,
splotch–skin–stripped to underwear in sudden sun,
and her worn braggadocio beside what's left
of a church, its earthbound gothic spire, striking.
Naked, she is mending what has served for a coat,
her needle hemming winter. Or across a center tram–rail,
one corpse floats its shoreline of flotsam,
was a white swan before, a bloat-big piece of a moving chill
that haunts the global, now. Or on her solid bench
our priestess hunches, and she stretches
her long dugs over her stitching.
She did not die this winter.
Here comes dogwood; pollen. Spring.

− 4 −

ON BREAKING

Pele's Dark Landing

Well, there are no leaves here either,
but I have imagined the garden.
So I'll tell my several hearts:

(And maybe we do not have only one, made to be
cracked like the sculpt of a woman's inner lips
on the floorwall of a cave we visit—inner, silverlong,
more giant than our life, and red with tarnish;

cracked again by the night's quake, feared of the dark
earth, famed,
now veined, and a little broken—

a sixty-three mile lava tube that skews from the moon-
scaped mount to the cooler sea—an imprint on the floor
of her hardened flow: ancient, raw, flying
vulva of the deity of all fires.)

Her legend smiles that she,
pursued by an overeager king and crouched in her innerworld,
hid, stooped there to plant love like a graffito.

There to leave her sign of womanhood and nothing else, there.
Walls of scrolled and jagged and sculpted flame-points, there.
Fervor or chase were not her whole desire, not from a king,
not from a fool, not from him, in fact, a conqueror.

So she left, to remember—

fictions of a passion to burst my hearts, darkness
to green a garden—a fact of myth, of woman.

We dozed above the molten... and under star quilts there,
as the earth broke night and morning and I laughed a little—
errant for love, for the ash of old cries,
for the plow of tears, even for conquerors.
Dreaming, I hissed at demons, in the several names of God.

There are gardens and there are not.
There is love and there is not. There are leaves and
there are not. But there is/was/ever...fire
and some god, some start and shape like a changed
autumnal blood...black imprint
of a garden, of an endlessly mended
woman, of love. *Pacem.*

To What is Broken

Neighbor to what is broken, kin to rain, how it wants
with all that wanting is—to be absorbed.
Kin to cats who sleep in crypts whose doors have been
removed because men were having sex within
those up-right rooms and families demanded better
treatment and cats benefited. Homeless in favorite
cemeteries, broken with sphinxes, armless with Venuses.

Could I hurry the dying that I might birth a woman of
knowing—she would wear black to the dance and boogey.
Never need a facelift, capable of making lullabies impromptu,
no need for love songs, and not dirges. She would know as little
as I do. But angels would step from monuments to know her better.
Broken things.

She'd write the lines that I do. Women climbing steps to home—
might suddenly remember them as prayers. She would make a town
of fixed things, carry paste in a pocket, peace in her breasts, homeless
gardens would open to her, instead of graves.

I need an umbrella that can't be broken by wind. A hope
that cannot be dismissed as futile, an end to grief. A town built
on knowing. A neighbor in my bed all long and thunderous night.

A river that ends when I say so.

FRESQUE TRANSPOSÉE

(d'après Sandro Botticelli's "L'Annonciation")

Like this, she seems to mime. Like this. And the mimic is so perfect
that we see the infant between those empty paws, her blue drapes such
that they could be holding holy ghost, already. Oh, our wish to hold
something holy. World, in its caul of killing as it is. Mother.

I kneel as child to mother, help me, to this master of a metaphor, *il
Signor Botticelli*. An annunciatory paint-poem, a magnificat: pregnant
Mary on her long wide angled plane—on the left, the angel hovers
in, its mask of such compassion to be bearer of such tiding as to stop
a world—as if it knows all alpha, all omega of the story—and the arms
and digits cross the levitated breast as if they would protect the same heart
that must speak.

Far, far right of the canvas, across an empty space of pillar and throned
bed, its single pillow, and veil, and veils, and marble floor, and space, and
space—a chicken-egg-shell-blue robed Mary tilts. She wears the sheer
Renaissance on her mane for veil, and isn't she the same redhead as Venus
in that other shell, birthing? Yes, Mary, here, nearly cradled too, in velum
—enacts her coming womb, its story.

She folds, half kneel and half a stance more *Quan Yin*—leaning in this one's
gown—her head, her torso to her right, while her hands edge left—and they
are empty, notably empty. Are miming their position that may, that will, that
must hold the child. What would I change, in any story?

On Hearing Pergolesi, a Friday Concerto

Not yet Easter now but dark,
but dusk, how this nearness of March-soprano
strays exposure, like old light—layered, and multiple.
This dust of the moon, breaking.

This is magnolia, in the courtyards,
and April, climbing the shoulder of its Stabat Mater
for a better view of joy, after.

This is the slow-hipped walk of winter's late fugue,
and the mimosa's promise.
This, the dust of the Hôtel Dieu
across its island of stone.

Still, a shoulder soft with Saturday's
desire, sips her warmed, day-drowning hour.
Soft, because skies, and copper light,
lost on its own thread.
Soft, because it bends into the Seine
like some redhead on a silken sheet, already
rumpled for her arrival
and His death.
Soft, because He hung by dust
and thread
and promise, and love.

And she mourned with her high voice
and for ever, layered, and multiple, and music, and mother.

OF GRACE

But it was Tuesday's child who's full of grace.
How do we dare compare
hells like hotel rooms of
grief,   its keeper?
The lost sound of a fountain
or ruin's painted table
with epiphanic noon—with light—light,
I know you, why are you making war too,
in a time of war, why useless, helpless ray,
are you rocking?

Put crimes' conspired fires on the same chance
plains with cries of luck and call it what, this time?
December.

Ghost, or peace in her transparency, or God
the thresher too on whom we called for peace,
thin metal dress and drummer—humming over coals,
these wars or vengeance waters had always been
within our chill and tilted stations of the possible,
breaking.
Prophets true to roost, perched—
seeds of their feeding time, scattered on our plain,
where should we gather,   gone the fountain?

At a little distance and long unburied
babies lain on sands like quiet fish for sale,
what to call day—endless in its swimming—
unconsecrated meal?   or unblessed wave?
unburied war?   December's child.   Nearer
than we have ever been to where we are.

Le Grand Veneur

In the stillest courtyard in creation where
Hesse's street ends at an angle with la rue
du Grand Veneur, a flock of twenty swallows'
silhouettes—climbs dawn, the viney garden.
Gated and trellised rose-fists lift their many
faiths, pink to light. Unmoving, all is well.

Where high ceilinged rooms, their drapes
still drawn make mirrors of the bird-swathes
and facing casement windows coiffed with
triangles like dunces' hats—sunrise,
from an eager sky. The roses are locked in,
it's early for freedom where I am stopped
like any vagabond for perfume and birdsong
—to open.

When it comes, before the church bells, call it
awe's morning.   Or last night, before I slept,
another woman's occasional lover
nuzzled my   yes, kissed   before   left my door where
we'll be circumspect, we must; his curve to me, *Quan
yin*, leaning.

Before a Vowel

Dying has a habit of running out of space. "Kutna Hora" —James Ragan

All our memoirs, hung over boulevards, and seas.
Lost beasts of the avenues, their fractured bleats, and rests.

After a last train, but before a vowel, a white cat, calling.
You've wondered whether the words die, as petals, as cats
in a fire.

Wondered if they live in quiet,
then, as poets walk with ashes.

Or old as the pigeon women
bear their age, as soldiers bear
their dead, the demented,
vowels knifed in their splayed
palms, broken winged, braying

wondered, whether the words die,
but the bird insists its song, noted
torn books, of the late burned air …

Door

Before another blatant hour, do not love a country;
it will turn you into a killer, defending your tree, your road,
your stars. Try not to protect the wren, its furred
babies. Say prove yourself to me again, I of doubt's
despair born deep in winter. Prove we are not born
in the cauls of killing.

Le Passage de la Main d'Or

Begging the air.
Gaping belly of the soul, now,
on her sidewalk knees, still,
left hand, cupped.

Damp stones are toning clothe yourself
in cotton dawn, in naked distance,
you have forgotten how to pray.
Know how the lovely stripes of the land snail
vanish when she dies. All color, then, forgotten.

Taste the racket of parrots, an immense green tribe
at sunrise. You know first light. You know how
good it is to stand bare breasts to morning. Know
the feathered vast of one cloud's hover.
The clarity of high wind, cleaning,
tide, its blood-weeds insisting.

Still begging.

I want to tell her this:
how I want to die again believing.
My stripes, forgotten.
I want to testify
how in stones I have known the faces
of the gods in every weather.
In a violin's high note in Le Passage
de la Main d'Or, a swathe of silk around
the thinning ribs of autumn.

I have dreamed my voice, stolen.

But in the traffic, crossing Quai de la Tournelle,

all its fallen, all its golden, what I am singing

sotto voce is

I want rapture for an hour. A better kiss.

November wine, turned water.

On Leaving Paradise

"Who am I then? His empty begging bowl"

We were calloused with the slate rivers of walking fast.

Not small, not consecrated, the boulevards of our bravery
stand apart,   hungry with their polished bones.

Talons. Handprints in a book of the dead.
Our nipples swollen soft with worry.

We were solitaires searching for a muse who had arms and a hard kiss.

We wore headlamps like coalminers.
Found the changing willows,
the April veins, the myrtle, its lost and listing sparrow,   sing for me,
sing,   speak to me,   please, speak.

The muse was not small, not holy,   it cried for the belly of God
and so did I.

I never take a journey without the night.

ALL NIGHT

My friend shifts from daughter of
flesh to one more of these daughters
of universe we are, mothers in their
party dresses rise, condolences are
not necessary, we know where we
wing, no trampoline will do it any
minute sooner than is possible, and
then, belonging, enter air, fluvial.

Or, discover one new garden hidden
behind Saint Deny's bell, and down
the rue de Turenne's dawn-stretch, stilled,
inside a courtyard walled with other
centuries, and doubled windows' reflect
of the east. Its gated rose and low nasturtium
vine ahead of sunrise. All the swallows
there—call on all

swallows—to ellipse eclipses, fly for
this necessary invocation of the daily
light, how else will we survive our
countries' uniforms of power, gray
immediate hours? Give us swallows,
hover, like urged wings everywhere,
preparing voice to overcome the hot
and breathless combats, all night.

COMMUNION

Let us come into communion.
The sea is sick of fish—randomly, it wants a god.

Black-weather bird, you are a scratch on silver. The scratch will not
be repaired, what use is polish?

Whom do you follow   after the falconer?
Across the field, bells hang in darkness braver than the stars.

Once bells could speak. Who silenced them once, lies quiet.

The Berlin wall stood built for twenty-eight years, its stones like
Jericho's, fell. Wall after wall after wall. When will our wall fall?

Be the bell.   Be the bell.
: that the hand of the prophet should let you fall when you are
most fervently at prayer and climbing. that the blue and golden chips
of the Alhambra are gifts, borne in the willing palms of revenants. Be
the bell and be the bell.

"Je garde / mon ange," mon Cocteau. Let us come into communion.

When will a chance wing randomly come in to save us, ever? How much
does it hurt? Who can count skin? Let us come in to communion.

On metro stairs where the redhead I know wears gloves to protect against
viruses, La Peau du Chagrin's poster—Skin of Sorrow—shouts.

On the street of deportations in the cold zone of our winter of memory, this
winter of memory, the neighbors are lined to nod to a barrel that contains

what remains of the days of skin the days of remembering the days of
killing kin that have never ended only changed skeletons, only changed skin

in a locked room writing one word, love, in water, on the walls.

—Mémorial des martyrs de la Déportation, Paris, France—

− 5 −

BEST LOVE

BEST LOVE AND GOODBYE

(a collage in many parts)

"Si le silence est l'envers du langage / la poésie est l'endroit du silence."—Michel Camus
– If silence be the inverse of language / poetry is the locus of silence. –

i

a

A woman readies for her Tuesday, practices tai chi in her mind, that the knife will be even, controlled, a crane, a slow tiger. A dance from which she awakens, a hungry crow, long afternoons, ahead.

A woman spending afternoons in Père Lachaise for twenty winters. Walking on soft mossed beds of those who are not famous.

Her familiar lives in a crypt, is black and furred and thin and grateful, her gifts to him are bits of liver. He will worry. Mourn, if he must.

b

This is not our youth. There have been infancies. Even seagulls can hide their bloodthirst, briefly.

If it never occurs, if this sun opposite the belly and the bookseller's stall and that other blonde in her urined shawls who talks to corners and walks not well, and the two on the corner who curl side by side as spoons on the night cement but beg on opposite sides of la rue de Rivoli. If each stops arguing. If each were resuscitated by day's even tempered clavichords of air.

c

But, we've begun. And it was battle that was the small lie, not heaven. Not its harbinger, peace, but doubt.

d

Doubt, as the scrawny black winged things of winter, doubt that though it turns a little warmer, sun will feed them. Doubt. In our youth this was where we waited with no cynicism, for blossoms. April would do what it was meant to, and the secret buds between our legs would imitate, remembering what love does.

e

We mount a pilgrimage toward delicate things. We walk on our knees while countries profess elements of surprise. We ask, will today be the closet of terrible things that was not unlocked?

f

Their bones muse, how flesh is possible. How can it breathe like old springtime on the eve of blood, oh call it a name, call it readying a veil, call it a war, our familiar.

g

If it will come, like the belladonna flower, drooping blossoms tinted hint of peach and wash of white and the poisoned drop that will find you, what color will it be? What did their branches know of destiny's crossed knees or broken rhyme?

h

We've seen the Imperial War Museum, in London. Tank, named devil. Gun, labeled versatile and efficient. Heard Siegfried Sassoon hiss, *does it matter...losing your legs?*

i

If it never happens. If there is no operation on Tuesday. If peace slides in like a lover on a virgin's sheet, not cruel not frightening, if sun will not move; if we will not need to bury or begin or name a shadow that has strangulation in its open busy hands. If we will not need to bury, or begin.

j

Wilfred Owen toned, *I lost all my earthly faculties and fought like an angel.* Winter white, a rose, before the war-door, dares to learn the climate.

I'm longing for a cut peach branch that a passerby is holding. Can't I have it? Pink small fragile thing like a Zen painting, its humble amputated limb of possibility shines. All over London, I would carry that pink.

Imagine my non existence. Best love and goodbye, Rupert Brooke.

ii

_____

_____

From the Malecon to the white
sharks, there are no bridges.
From the ice floe in a Medici fountain
to sweat pools between Havana's
breast bones—there is sky; an only
bridge that may not lie.

There may be savagery as usual, cloaked in justice as usual. In one place there must be elephants, pawing. In another, baby Oona's barbie doll, dismembered while she sings to it. A melodic line her *maman* does at bedtime. It is not bedtime. It will never be bedtime again, if it begins.

————————————————

Opposite of silence, the ash tree.
Opposite of hate, peace, quietly, in a time of war.
How many wars are in the collective memory? I don't remember.
When can I write the poem without the word whore in it. I said war but I am corrected because I have once again complained.

The Seine! yelps a toddler girl from her stroller. Her *maman* beams at one so young.

You're thinner and more beautiful coos her mirror, when it breaks.

Every passage is worthy of the soul's grief. She is always gluing her pieces.

————————————————

...but an infection of the common sky.
                    —Robert Graves.

————————————————

Before and After visiting the 400 Doomed Youth
soldier poets of that other century
A man who wants our response to the new Holocaust
wing: Is it an attraction, he needs to know

Time Out London: Daily, 10 — 4 Visitors can listen to broadcasts made by Churchill, Chamberlain, Roosevelt, Hitler, or take refuge from a London blitz. In an Anderson shelter, an evocative mockup. Gray and gray an hour rides the Thames like a ferry for Lethe. Melancholic baby sphinx, what bird-skull loves your ungrown paw, what questions. Knowing a thing's name is wizard's purview, magic, world without end without reply, amen.

Let the tangled briar and thorns and dry branch—remind me. I do not wish. Winds, do not die this night. London's most controversial immigrants are being sent home. The anatomical exhibition of real human bodies has a last admission at 9 pm.

The man with a cart is giving away cut branches, their exciting adolescent eruptions of unopened blossom pink. Oh, I desire one.

There are Buddhists, massed to chant and cultivate an inner garden, as a precaution. In Britain, the majority of Buddhists are artists, they say. How can that Saint James Square pelican be so individual, look at his elbows. There he is amid that lower order, swans, and battle, so near, again. At the Imperial War Museum, small boys and daddies touch the skins of tanks. *Soft, daddy, soft. Strong, daddy, strong.* Dead as Wilfred Owen.

Wasted cries.

When can we be passionate about a mountain or a rice-bird again? When will the sword of kisses pierce my nipples perfectly as readied bombs and legs, none, hands, none, babies born for that and nothing more

(?)

I hope it won't injure your poetry. Be good. —Robert Graves

There is no war yet.

Soon.

———————————————

"Nothing has changed me," the man with African bones answered what I had asked him. I am patient. I wait."

———————————————

Her father did not stutter on his last breaths, she said. He held
the last color blue like the peacock's tail, disintegrating all
iridescence.

Say there is no war no color no fan of
bravery, nothing wrong, ever.

Not even the histories of lands beyond these sadnesses
seems to convince claws to be kinder. They have been
promised what is pink and will
never blossom.

Who would have kissed the tatters? Only to not do it badly.
A draft of a cry, crumpled, could be discovered in a river.

———————————————

iii

But it has begun.

The sharp news breaks our step and sleep.
This undressed chapter, this naked barking.
If sons come home wrongly glued,
Saint Theresa, walk barefoot with us, now.

Before shipping out this week, United States servicemen are leaving deposits in sperm
banks. One California bank is offering a storage discount. One soldier will say: for
every person in the world who has not and will not harm me and my family, I likewise
vow not to harm them and theirs.

Go, darling. Do it for us.

———————————————

If mortality is your enemy and you do not understand it, why not go to the expert?
                                                                    —*Margaret Atwood*

———————————————

At Père Lachaise, for rest, born into a war's mouth, the sparrow
Madame Lambankas, *dite Edith Piaf*, sings yet, and spits her five foot sorrow.

It has begun.

Macduff's children, all slaughtered.
Ours, about to be, or worse, theirs.

It is cold, this season in Paris; tulips, trying to stand upright.
On Proust, a single pink long stem,
tries.

A stone, around this need.

I wrap us in the odor of bees.

Who does not like dying, come.
A stone around this need, drinking the ocean.

I've dined with the pride in the sincerity of soldiers.
A stone around this poor dream, let it drown.

Everyone is cold.
We could feel the desert's steam, stiffening.
Ghosts of soldiers who are not soldiers yet because their
war has not begun; tears, dry as taped butterflies.

A stone around this need is drinking the ocean.
Who does not like dying, come.

I fish. I fish with these hands, with this soul.
Wrap me in the odor of bees.

My nightmares are men with medals, pride, in the sincerity of soldiers.
A stone around the dream that they will drown.

Who does not like heroes, come.   The desert's stiffening.   The weary camels under
their trillion stars. I will not weep when I remember Zion. I will not stack pebbles.

When rats come think of camels under stars and not alone.   Think of stones, drinking
the ocean. The bees are watching us, with all their fear.   We were waiting for an
announcement, that forsythia might grow golden even in the light of grief, that year.

---

iv

A global angst the color of black pearl.

Two women too old to find new men
in the incomprehensible social sea, we
are coral, hard backed, we have this terrible
wish to redesign the species.

In Dakar, they drown. They would have given three bags of rice for a drowned
college-bound brain.

O call it, will it come, incautious beast? Yes, certainly, it has claws.

In the islands of Malaysia, they say that "absence presupposes presence."

War is frightening us. Very soon I want so desperately to love that I
have grown a garden of weeds, an ability to worship.

Pinks again. A gypsy's hand as weary with begging
as I with war. Weary? It has not even been declared.
Weary I say.

Expectation is a biochemical weapon.

Who would bury?

Gray uniforms in all their deserts, as ready to spit pink before dying as
a dead boy can see where fathers have steered his kin, how kissing
the ground, calling it "mine," is the very sin. Where he lies is
your country   & mine.   It is unique.   In its insects,   crawling for cover.

———————————————

I have a box of Lobelia, tumbling blue blooms in the window,
it waits for water,
how else can it or will it discover abundance? Cicadas. Benediction.
C'est une bénédiction de faire votre connaissance, madame.
That is why I loved him.

Bamboo, rounded high and striped with a single green thin line
of marking, can bend and not break. My vagabond soul, in a red dress,
this time. A dire hope for creation, not updated. After. Against. Although.
Among. As. All. As if. Ah. Please, together, say   Ah

that the knife will be even, controlled, a crane, a slow tiger.

★

—March, 2003—

Who Were Those Pretty

Our teacher was dying, but that was wisdom, its broken
wing; we could fix it: colorless glue, new soup, new children.

We were pretty women then, bad love but unbound long hair,
how it knew our hard waists. We knew the great mountain-

wind that could kill or kiss from a tropical hill; we knew
the indiscriminate scent of fallen owls.

Night jasmine tugged our wills in my headless red jeep, its slow
rust, insouciant of the white rain, our slower aging.

Five billion nights of fixing. The repaired sky hangs loose
as old men's flesh. How being a human invokes ritual, grief

for spiritual breakage, do I mean breakthrough? Nothing will help you
brace for the broken mind, the fall of the fair jester, the too sad man
in a Paris chair, wailing. Nothing will help you sew solace into the skin.

Our hope is torn from the scrape of God's womb.
Bless the broken, scars, all over this sky.

In the Luxembourg garden today, Iegor says the goddess Sita cared not
if she was a sow or a queen or a mollusk in her next life. Only, let her praise.

On iced Wednesdays before Christmas, I was supposed to learn from that.
I always study dying, its polar borning, at Christmas.
I was thinking I must run away to naked cliffs, to mumbling birds, to another God.

Bless the bald Medici Garden, its ripped out reds and purples, all their chilled roots. Bless my loosening hold; my upper arms warble,

in their silken nightgown, soft as crying and the folding sky.

How it will wait with us: sky, and our soiled laundry. sky, and our sliced bread. Will it forgive us for not being crazy? for hunger? for bleach? for failing?

★

Will you wake for me again?

the lost bells cry in sleep…

—Jerome Rothenberg

Notes:

* The opening epigraph, "Out of the wilderness of possibility comes a vine without a name," by William Stafford, is from his acceptance speech for the National Book Award in 1963.

* The closing quotation, "Will you wake for me again? / the lost bells cry in sleep..." is from "Poems for the Game of Silence" by Jerome Rothenberg, "for Diane, A Slower Music."

* – 1 –

* "Long Drum"—*Linaria Cymbalaria*—a flowering ivy, some of its folk names are Mother of thousands, Madonna's herb, Wandering Jew, White goddess, toad flax, Ruin of Rome.

* "In Progress"—*les hiboux* are owls.

* "Unbreakable Umbilicus,"—the room with six griefs was inspired from a poem by Jane Hirschfield.

* – 2 –

Louise Bourgeois is a pioneer artist of the 20th & 21st centuries.

* "Of Days"—Snow Queen, Freya, Hel, Santa Muerte, Oya, Maman Brigitte are some of the mythic, ancient names for death. Santeria's Oya brings storms in her colored rags; Haiti's Maman Brigitte is sometimes pictured with her tree, a weeping willow.

* – 3 –

"The Story," "After The End After The Beginning," "The Vehicle," were written in Aceh, Sumatra, following the tsunami of December 2004. I had gone there to work in a survivor's clinic.

* *"To learn how to die, watch cherry blossoms, observe chrysanthemums,"* epigraph to "The Story," Anonymous, 1700, translated by Sam Hamill.

* "Cain—After" is, in its way, a midrash—a telling after Cain slew Abel, Chapter 4, Genesis. My thanks to the poet Alicia Ostriker, for teaching me the word.

* *"Who am I then? His empty begging bowl..."* epigraph to "On Leaving Paradise," translated by Sam Hamill from Rumi.

* *Le Passage De La Main D'Or* may translate as "the way of the golden hand." It is also one of the alleyways in the heart of Paris.

★ These lines in the poem "Un-titled," are from Shakespeare's "*King Lear*," *Act-iv. sc.-iv*

> "*All blest secrets,*
> *All you unpublished virtues of the earth,*
> *Spring with my tears! be aidant and remediate*
> *In the good man's distress! Seek, seek for him*
> *Lest his ungoverned rage dissolve the life*
> *That wants the means to lead it.*"

Saint Lucy is often called patron saint of the blind. My reference is to Lucy's iconic dish of eyes.

"Un-titled" was written following the devastations in New Orleans in Summer 2005.

★ "To Autumn"—Kalua (Papa Kalua Kaiahua) was a modern practitioner of the art of spiritual traditional healing in the Hawaiian islands. Empedocles became known as a Daimon, pre-Socratic Sicilian shaman who first conceived of four elements, earth, air, fire, water.

★ – 4 –

"Je garde / mon ange," mon Cocteau, means literally "I keep my angel," my Cocteau—as if speaking to Jean Cocteau with his words. The poem "communion," was written on the sixtieth anniversary of the Soviet Army's liberation of Auschwitz.

★ – 5 –

"Best Love and Goodbye"—Père Lachaise is the Parisian cemetery of famous, infamous, and pilgrim.

"*C'est une bénédiction de faire votre connaissance, madame,*"—It is a blessing to meet you, madame.

★

My deep gratitude to the poets Marie Ponsot, Marilyn Hacker, Stanley Moss, Cyrus Cassells, Jerome Rothenberg, Alice Notley, Mary Baine Campbell, Jim Ragan. Kathleen Spivack, Robin Lim, for each one's caring reading of my poems during their growing.

Each poet, each breaking—teaches me the word.

★

Acknowledgements

I am grateful to the editors of the following publications in which poems from this book first appeared (some in earlier versions):

Chelsea, [Recipient of The Chelsea Award] "In Progress," "But a Passage in Wilderness," "Walking Papers," "Who Were Those Pretty," "Le Grand Veneur," "All Night." *Nimrod International*, "Best Love & Goodbye," *Van Gogh's Ear*, [& recipient of Robert H. Winner Award,] "The Geese Are Back," *Poetry International*, "Lautrec, I've Heard Shot Spiders," "After the End After the Beginning," "The Story." *Another Chicago Magazine*, "Holy as a Bird," "Passages to Mourn," "The Vehicle." *Kalliope*, "Un-titled" *Pool*, "communion," *Runes*, "On Leaving Paradise," *Southern California Anthology* & *100 Poets Against the War*, "Equinox, Africa," *Rattapallax*, "This Sentence" & "Pele's Dark Landing," *Paris/Atlantic*, "Every Afternoon;" *BigCityLit.com*, "On Hearing Pergolesi, a Friday Concerto" *Women's Studies Quarterly*, "On Frailty;" *Poetry Society of America 2002 Awards Program*, "This Sentence."

Sincere thanks to Jean-Marc Eldin for his always beautiful eye for book design. My thanks for friends, and for half-angels.

About the Author

MARGO BERDESHEVSKY was born in New York City in 1945. She currently lives in Paris. For many years, she lived in the Hawaiian islands. A graduate of the High School of Performing Arts, she attended Northwestern and New York Universities, quit, for a role in her first Off Broadway play; she was trained as an actress by Lee Strasberg. She performed in the world premiere of Harold Pinter's *The Basement* & *Tea Party*, David Hare's *Slag*, worked in the companies of Lincoln Center and Joseph Papp's Public Theatre, toured the USA as Ophelia, and was nominated for a television Emmy award, for a country western drama in which she had her head in an oven, but was saved by a neighbor who prayed for her.

Her honors include the Robert H. Winner Award from the Poetry Society of America (selected by Marie Ponsot,) the *Chelsea* Poetry Award, *Kalliope's* Sue Saniel Elkind Award, places in the Pablo Neruda and Ann Stanford Awards (selected by Yusef Komunyakaa,) and Border's Books/ *Honolulu Magazine* Grand Prize for Fiction, and 4 Pushcart Prize nominations for works in many of the leading literary journals, including *Agni*, *The Kenyon Review*, *The Southern Review*, *New Letters*, *Poetry International*, *Runes*, *Siècle 21*, *Europe*. Her Tsunami Notebook of poems and photographs was made following a journey to Sumatra in spring 2005, to work in a survivors' clinic in Aceh. A book of her short fictions, *Beautiful Soon Enough*, and *Vagrant*, a poetic novel, are now at the gate. The cover art for *But a Passage in Wilderness* is one of her montages.